CONTENTS

The Bad Luck of KING FRED

CHAPTER 1

King Frederick von Applegate III was very superstitious. He would never open an umbrella inside the palace and, everywhere he went, he carried with him a horseshoe, two four-leaf clovers (which made eight cloves in all), and his lucky penny. He would never walk under a ladder, or get out on the wrong side of the bed. And he never ever could hear anybody sneeze without saying "gesundheit".

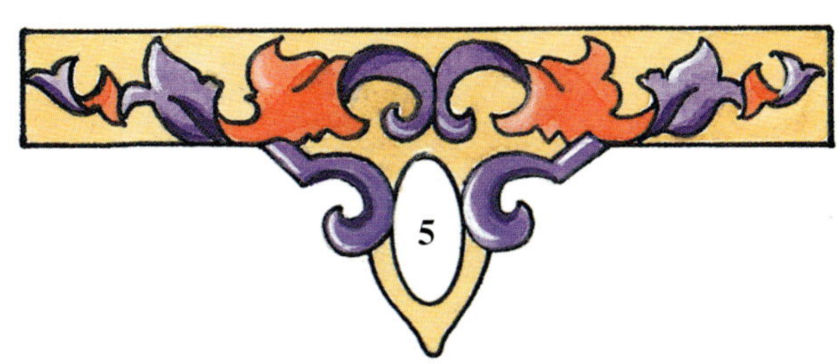

One day the king was sitting up in bed, enjoying his porridge. As he reached for his spoon, his new royal adviser burst through the door, which caused the king's hand to jerk and knock over the salt-cellar.

"Oh no, Your Majesty! It's terribly bad luck to spill salt. You must throw some over your left shoulder if you are to avoid total ruin," cried the adviser.

King Fred quickly did as the adviser cautioned, but he worried about whether he had been fast enough to avoid the cloud of doom. "There's nothing harder to get rid of than bad luck once you've got it," King Fred mourned.

He thought a bit, then said, "Make a royal proclamation that from now on all salt is to be banned from the kingdom. That will protect my subjects from the danger of spilling any."

"At once, Your Majesty," the adviser vowed, as he bowed from the room.

King Fred finished his porridge and began his morning brush-up. Every day, he bathed in the royal bath, shaved his royal chin, and waxed his royal moustache.

He had just risen from his bath, and was busy lathering his face when the adviser burst in once again. Startled, King Fred's hand knocked over his shaving mirror, causing it to smash on the bathroom floor.

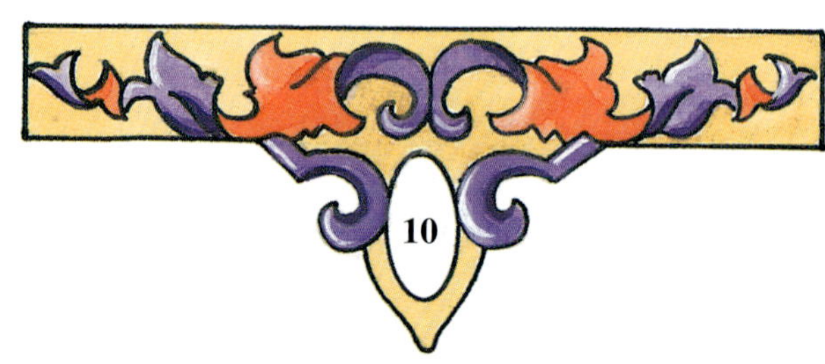

"Oh no, Your Majesty! This is total ruin! Breaking a mirror dooms you to seven years of bad luck!" the adviser cried.

"Seven years!" King Fred gulped. "Drat! The bad luck I have from spilling the salt has now stretched into seven years. Oh dear, oh dear, oh dear."

He sat down on the side of the bath and shook his head. "Oh, Adviser, we must protect my people from such a fate. Make another royal proclamation that, from now on, all mirrors are to be banned from the kingdom."

"At once, Your Majesty," the adviser vowed, as he bowed out of the room.

King Fred was now very sad and worried, and took no delight in dressing in his favourite blue uniform. He even forgot to wax his moustache, which was drooping slightly at the ends. Before his unlucky morning, he'd really been looking forward to visiting the kingdom's brand new mill.

Now, however, he found his steps dragging as he approached the royal coach.

"Oh no, Your Majesty!" cried the adviser, as he scrambled down the steps. "You stepped on a crack and broke your mother's back!"

King Fred was indeed standing on a crack. If his mother had still been alive, he could have really hurt her. He was relieved that his mother's back was in no danger.

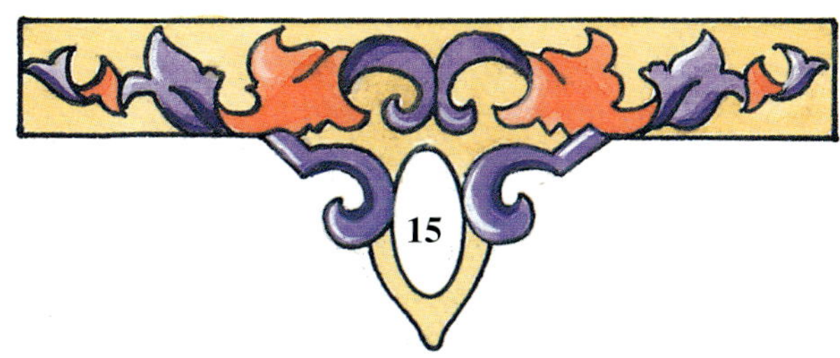

But he thought of all the other mothers in his kingdom whose backs could be broken so easily by thoughtless children.

"It's time for another proclamation, Adviser. From now on, all roads are to be ripped up so that there will be no more cracks that can break mothers' backs," King Fred announced tiredly.

"At once, Your Majesty," the adviser vowed.

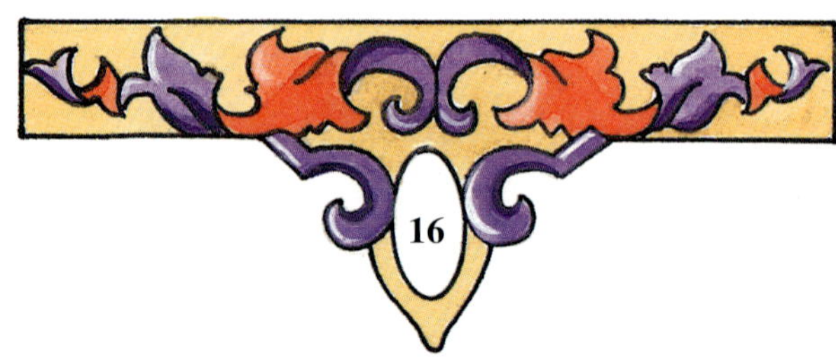

Hear Ye!
Hear Ye!

Let it be known that from
this day forward cracks in
the road are banned from
the kingdom by Royal Order
of King Fred.

"And now I shall return to my room and spend the rest of the day in bed before I do any more harm to myself, or my subjects, with all of this bad luck."

"As you please, Your Majesty," the adviser vowed, as the king went back up the steps.

CHAPTER 2

The next morning, King Fred was very miserable. The night before, a violent thunderstorm had raged for hours and hours, shaking the palace walls and pounding the palace roof.

Even worse, his bed was full of the salt he had thrown over his shoulder. No matter how much he brushed off the sheets, there was still enough left to scratch his skin.

He heard tapping at the door. It was the royal gardener. After hearing of the king's woes, she had brought King Fred another four-leaf clover, because twelve cloves are always better than eight. King Fred was very relieved. Surely the new clover would break his run of bad luck.

He felt a little better when the servant arrived with his breakfast tray. King Fred dug the spoon into his favourite porridge and scooped up a mouthful. The hot cereal rolled over his tongue and down his throat.

He started to smack his lips, then paused. Something was not quite right. He took a smaller spoonful and tried the porridge again. There was no flavour. The porridge tasted like warm paste.

The king pushed the tray aside and called for the royal cook. Within minutes, the cook shuffled through the door, wringing his hands in his apron and bobbing his head up and down.

King Fred said, "Something is wrong. My porridge tastes like paste."

"I'm sorry, Your Majesty. I made it just as I always do, but I didn't add salt because yesterday you forbade the use of it."

"Humph. You mean salt made the difference?" When the cook nodded nervously, King Fred said, "Well, it was time for a change, anyway. From now on, I'll just have something simple for breakfast like... toast."

The cook bowed out of the room, saying, "Very good, Your Majesty. Your wish is always my command, Your Majesty."

King Fred threw back the covers and went into the bathroom. His bath did much to restore his humour, but after he lathered his face, he found it very difficult to shave without a mirror.

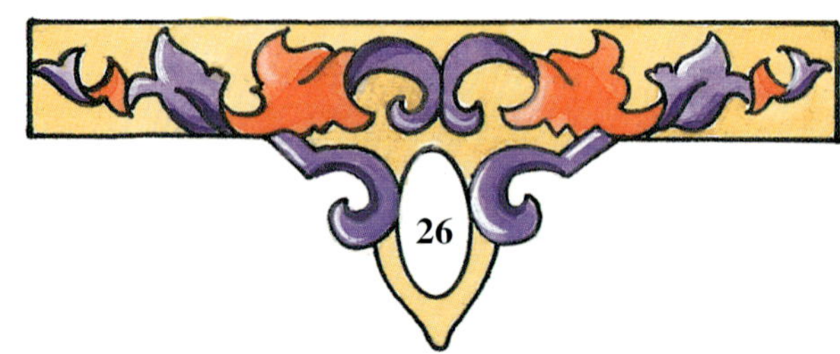

So much so, in fact, that he nicked himself thirteen times. It was also impossible to twist his moustache into the proper curl without a mirror. All he could manage was a lopsided corkscrew.

King Fred perked up again when he dressed in his second favourite green uniform, and went out to his coach to go on the postponed mill visit.

He hadn't gone very far when the coach wheels squelched to a stop. He rapped on the ceiling and called to his driver.

"Yes, Your Majesty?"

"Why have we stopped?" King Fred asked grumpily.

"Well, Your Majesty, because
all the roads have been ripped up to
get rid of any cracks, there is only
earth left for the surface. The storm
last night didn't help much either.
As you can see, we are firmly stuck
in the mud."

No matter which way the horses heaved, the coach barely moved. They were, indeed, stuck. King Fred ruined his second favourite uniform and boots walking through the sloppy, muddy mire back to the palace.

Chapter 3

When the muddy, grumpy, droopy-moustached king entered the Grand Hall, a black cat leapt down from a window sill and padded over to meet him.

"Oh no, Your Majesty!" the adviser cried. "A black cat crossing your path is the worst of bad luck. You must get rid of it immediately."

"*What?* Get rid of Snookums?"

"Of course, Your Majesty! You'll never have good luck if you don't!"

King Fred then stroked his chin and thought about the events of the day. He winced slightly when a finger touched one of the shaving nicks. He remembered the tasteless porridge. Then he looked down at his ruined uniform, which had been his second favourite.

"Adviser, I think it is time for another proclamation. From now on, the royal adviser is to be banished from the kingdom."

"At once, Your Maj..., I mean, Your Majesty! I cannot banish myself," the adviser said.

"No, but I can. I'm happy to say your presence is no longer required in this kingdom."

"But, Your Majesty, I only advised you for your own good."

"You had me get rid of salt, and mirrors, and roads, and now you want me to get rid of Snookums. She comes from a long line of mousers. Besides, she's my kitty cat. Now be gone! And never darken our doorstep again."

The guards dragged out the not-so-royal adviser, who cried, "Oh no!"

King Fred bent down and picked up his cat.

"He was a very bad adviser, Snookums. I simply can't have him spreading his ideas all over my kingdom. After all, a person makes their own good luck."

Snookums seemed to agree, for her purring grew louder and louder.

King Frederick reversed all of the previous day's proclamations.

He threw away his horseshoe, the three four-leaf clovers (all twelve cloves), and put the lucky penny in his piggy bank.

Best of all, he never again let superstitions rule his life, although he still said "gesundheit" whenever somebody sneezed. After all, it was the polite thing to do.

THE SUPERSTITIONS OF KING FRED

Many of the superstitions that King Fred believed in are actually hundreds of years old.

Umbrellas

In the past, people used umbrellas as protection from the sun. Long ago, in parts of Asia, opening an umbrella in the shade – and especially in the house – was considered an insult to the power of the sun and brought bad luck.

Four-Leaf Clovers

Most clover grows with three leaves to a stem. From time to time, a four-leaf clover will grow. Because this doesn't happen very often, a person who finds a four-leaf clover is considered lucky.

Walking Under a Ladder

Walking under a ladder is bad luck because paint or tools might fall on you. It is also bad luck because you might cause the person on the ladder to fall off. Long ago in England, condemned prisoners were made to walk under the gallows ladder before they were hanged. Now that *is* bad luck!

Saying "Gesundheit"

Everyone knows that when a person gets a cold, they sneeze a lot. Once, people believed sneezing was a sure sign of serious illness. That is why the custom began of saying things like "gesundheit" or "salud" – which mean "good health to you" – to protect the person from the bad luck of getting sick.

Broken Mirrors

Breaking a mirror is supposed to be bad luck because long ago some people believed that if you looked into a mirror you could see your future. If you broke that mirror, your future would be broken, too.

Black Cats

Over the years, many people have been scared of things "that go bump in the night". Black cats, which can creep through the night unseen and unheard, were considered bad luck, especially if they crossed your path.

From the Author and Illustrator

When I was little, my father read us Irish folktales, and stories about Robin Hood. As I grew older, I made up my own bedtime stories before falling asleep. I still tell myself stories, but now someone pays me to write them down!

Anna-Maria Crum

ALL THE WORLD'S A STAGE
All the World's a Stage!
Which Way, Jack?
The Bad Luck of King Fred
Famous Animals
Puppets
The Wish Fish

WILD AND WONDERFUL
Winter Survival
Peter the Pumpkin-Eater
Because of Walter
Humphrey
Hairy Little Critters
The Story of Small Fry

FRIENDS AND FRIENDSHIP
Uncle Tease
PS I Love You, Gramps
Friendship in Action
Midnight Rescue
Nightmare
You Can Canoe!

ACTION AND ADVENTURE
Dinosaur Girl
Amelia Earhart
Taking to the Air
No Trouble at All!
River Runners
The Midnight Pig

Written by **Anna-Maria Crum**
Illustrated by **Anna-Maria Crum**
Edited by **Rebecca McEwen**
Designed by **Pat Madorin**

02 01 00 99 98 97
10 9 8 7 6 5 4 3 2 1

Published by Shortland Publications Limited, 2B Cawley Street,
Ellerslie, Auckland, New Zealand
Distributed in Australia by Rigby Heinemann, a division of
Reed International Books Australia Pty Ltd. ACN 001 002 357,
22 Salmon Street, Port Melbourne, Victoria 3207
Distributed in the United Kingdom by Kingscourt Publishing Limited,
P.O. Box 1427, Freepost, London W6 9BR

Printed by Colorcraft, Hong Kong
ISBN: 1-57257-731-2